GRAMMAR MADE EASY

GRAMMAR MADE EASY

Adjectives and Adverbs

Merlene J. Purkiss

MJP Publishing
Miami, FL

Copyright © 2016 MJP Publishing Company

All Rights Reserved.

No part of this book may be reproduced or transmitted in any form or by any means, electronic or mechanical, including photocopying and recording, or by any information storage or retrieval system without the prior written permission of the copyright owner unless such copying is expressly permitted by federal copyright law.

Please direct all correspondence to:
MJP Publishing Company
P.O. Box 162098
Miami, FL 33116-2098
mjp.publishing@gmail.com

ISBN: 978-1-63452-870-2
Library of Congress Control Number: 2016910978

First printing July 2016

Printed in the U.S.A.

Contents

ADJECTIVES 7
   Exercise 1 7
   Exercise 2 8
   Exercise 3 9
   Exercise 4 9
Comparative and Superlative Adjectives 11
Adjectives with One Syllable 11
Adjectives Ending in -y 11
Adjectives with More Than One Syllable 12
Irregular Adjectives 12
   Exercise 5 13
   Exercise 6 13
   Exercise 7 14
   Exercise 8 15
Demonstrative Adjectives 16
   Exercise 9 16
Articles *a*, *an*, *the* as Adjectives 17
   Exercise 10 18
   Exercise 11 19

ADVERBS 21

Common Adverbs 21

Changing Adverbs into Adjectives 21

Exercise 12 22

Exercise 13 22

Comparative and Superlative Adverbs 24

Exercise 14 24

Commonly Confused Adverbs: Good and Well 25

Exercise 15 25

Exercise 16 26

REVIEW 28

About the Author 34

Adjectives and Adverbs

Adjectives

Adjectives can only be used to describe nouns or pronouns.

Adjective	Noun
red	house
white	car
beautiful	girl
handsome	guy
high	mountain
black	dog
responsible	person
big	church
new	car
incredible	woman

EXERCISE 1   Underline the **adjective(s)** in each sentence.

Example: This student is <u>intelligent</u>.

1. I cannot afford a new computer.

2. The loud noise from the music keeps me awake.

3. The delicious spaghetti was prepared by my neighbor.

4. It was a good idea to visit Cassandra.

5. Juan broke the small window close to his bedroom.

6. We should prepare for the dangerous hurricane.

7. The tiny baby can crawl.

8. Felix is a good driver.

9. Fabian thinks Manny is a silly man.

10. I went to an interesting movie last night.

EXERCISE 2 Fill in the blank with an appropriate **adjective**.

Example: Is Francisco a **responsible** person?

1. Is Martin a .... mechanic?

2. Does Raymond live in a .... house?

3. Johnny is a .... student.

4. Do you go to a .... church?

5. Is Fred a .... guy?

6. Is this a .... mountain?

7. Francisco is an .... person?

8. Paulina has .... hair.

9. Is this a .... movie?

10. Maria is a .... cook.

Grammar Made Easy

EXERCISE 3 Find an appropriate **adjective** to describe each of the following **nouns**.

Example: black dog

1. .... man
2. .... movie
3. .... dress
4. .... house
5. .... apple
6. .... teacher
7. .... car
8. .... cat
9. .... woman
10. .... building

EXERCISE 4 Answer these questions with **yes** or **no** responses.

Examples: Is Mary an **intelligent** girl?
Yes, she is an **intelligent** girl.
No, she is not an intelligent girl.

1. Does Alfredo have a **big** house?

   ....

2. Is Carlton a **competent** mechanic?

   ....

Adjectives and Adverbs

3. Do you drive a **blue** car?

   ....

4. Is Robert a **new** student?

   ....

5. Do you have **many** friends?

   ....

6. Do you like **yellow** paint?

   ....

7. Is Marcie a **foreign** student?

   ....

8. Are these **ripe** tomatoes?

   ....

9. Can you climb **high** mountains?

   ....

10. Did Maria buy a **fancy** dress?

    ....

Comparative and Superlative Adjectives

Use the **comparative –er** to compare **two** persons or things, and use the **superlative –est** to compare **three** or **more** persons or things.

Adjectives with One Syllable

For all **one-syllable** adjectives, use **–er** to form the **comparative** and **–est** to form the **superlative**.

Adjective	Comparative	Superlative
tall	tall**er**	tall**est**
big	bigg**er**	bigg**est**
large	larg**er**	larg**est**
high	high**er**	high**est**
black	black**er**	black**est**
young	young**er**	young**est**
red	redd**er**	redd**est**
slow	slow**er**	slow**est**
fat	fatt**er**	fatt**est**
white	whit**er**	whit**est**

Adjectives Ending in –y

For **two-syllable** adjectives ending in **–y**, drop the **–y** and add **–ier** to form the **comparative** and **–iest** to form the **superlative**.

Adjective	Comparative	Superlative
happy	happ**ier**	happ**iest**
funny	funn**ier**	funn**iest**
pretty	prett**ier**	prett**iest**
silly	sill**ier**	sill**iest**
ugly	ugl**ier**	ugl**iest**
rocky	rock**ier**	rock**iest**
crazy	craz**ier**	craz**iest**
dirty	dirt**ier**	dirt**iest**
easy	eas**ier**	eas**iest**
sunny	sunn**ier**	sunn**iest**

Adjectives with More Than One Syllable

Use **more** to form the **comparative** and **most** to form the **superlative** of **adjectives** with **more than one syllable**.

Adjective	Comparative	Superlative
intelligent	**more** intelligent	**most** intelligent
difficult	**more** difficult	**most** difficult
beautiful	**more** beautiful	**most** beautiful
careful	**more** careful	**most** careful
handsome	**more** handsome	**most** handsome
persistent	**more** persistent	**most** persistent
contrary	**more** contrary	**most** contrary
yellow	**more** yellow	**most** yellow
knowledgeable	**more** knowledgeable	**most** knowledgeable
important	**more** important	**most** important

Irregular Adjectives

Adjective	Comparative	Superlative
good	better	best
bad	worse	worst
little	less	least
much	more	most

EXERCISE 5 Underline the correct **comparative** or **superlative** form of the adjective in parentheses.

1. Is this a (better, best) idea than yours?

2. What is the (more important, most important) step in changing a tire?

3. Flora bought the (more expensive, most expensive) car on the lot.

4. Fanny is the (funnier, funniest) comedian on television.

5. Of the three speakers, who is the (most eloquent, more eloquent) one?

6. Frank has the (worst, worse) eating habits in his family.

7. Who is the (richer, richest) person in America?

8. Of the two writers, Floyd is the (most interesting, more interesting) one.

9. Send me your (more efficient, most efficient) worker.

10. Of the three pieces of cake, Carlos chose the (biggest, bigger) piece.

EXERCISE 6 Answer these questions with **yes** or **no** responses.

Example: Is Sammy **taller** than Frank?
Yes, Sammy is **taller** than Frank.
No, Sammy is not **taller** than Frank.

1. Would Efrain make a **better** baseball player than Jason?

   ....

2. Does Mary have a **bigger** house than Fredrica?

   ....

Adjectives and Adverbs

3. Is Sylvia the **most intelligent** person in her class?

   ....

4. Is Melissa a **worse** math student than Keith?

   ....

5. Is Sage **taller** than Richard?

   ....

6. Is Ana **happier** than her sister?

   ....

EXERCISE 7 Use the following **adjectives** to form the **comparative** and **superlative**. The first one is done for you.

	Adjective	Comparative	Superlative
1.	young	younger	youngest
2.	marvelous	....	....
3.	silly	....	....
4.	common	....	....
5.	bad	....	....
6.	hot	....	....
7.	responsible	....	....
8.	beautiful	....	....
9.	intelligent	....	....
10.	great	....	....

EXERCISE 8 Underline the correct **adjective** in parentheses.

1. Frank is (taller, tallest) than his brother.

2. Of all the boys on the football team, Javier is the (better, best).

3. Mercury is the (hotter, hottest) of all the planets.

4. Simon is known as the (smarter, smartest) student in the class.

5. Is May the (wetter, wettest) month of the year?

6. Which is the (larger, largest) planet?

7. Miriam is the (worse, worst) singer in the contest.

8. Is Mars (driest, drier) than Earth?

9. Of the two girls, Maria is the (more, most) beautiful.

10. Is Mount Everest the (higher, highest) mountain?

11. The Bible is known as the (most, more) read book in the world.

12. Of all the players on the team, who is the (better, best)?

Demonstrative Adjectives

A *demonstrative adjective* is used to demonstrate or signal to the person or thing being referred to.

Examples: **this** man   **that** idea

   these books   **those** women

EXERCISE 9   Answer these questions with **yes** or **no** responses.

Example: Does **this** book belong to Frank?
Yes, **this** book belongs to Frank.
No, **this** book does not belong to Frank.

1. Are **those** papers yours?

   ....

2. Is **that** man your father?

   ....

3. Are **these** cars for sale?

   ....

4. Is **this** idea yours?

   ....

5. Are **these** dresses yours?

   ....

Articles a, an, the as Adjectives

Use *a* before words that begin with a ***consonant***: **b, c, d, f, g, h, j, k, l, m, n, p, q, r, s, t, v, w, x, y, z**.

Examples:　　**a** man　　　　**a** dog

　　　　　　　　a king　　　　**a** woman

　　　　　　　　a book　　　　**a** table

Use *an* before words that begin with a ***vowel***: (**a, e, i, o, u**).

Examples:　　**an** idea　　　　**an** apple

　　　　　　　　an orange　　　**an** egg

　　　　　　　　an ugly dog　　**an** hour (the ***h*** is silent)

Exceptions: Use a before words that begin with u but have a y sound:

　　　　　　　　a universe　　　**a** university

　　　　　　　　a unit　　　　　**a** union

　　　　　　　　a unicorn　　　**a** uniform

Use *the* with both consonants and vowels.

Examples:　　**The** apple is red.　　　**The** house is red.

　　　　　　　　The man is my friend.　**The** elephant is huge.

　　　　　　　　The tomato is green.　　**The** orange is sweet.

Adjectives and Adverbs

EXERCISE 10 Fill in the blank with *a* or *an*.

Examples: . . . . friend is a treasure.
A friend is a treasure.

Sammy has . . . . idea.
Sammy has an idea.

1. . . . . dog barks.

2. Johnny is . . . . good friend.

3. Francisco bought . . . . new car.

4. Samantha is . . . . incredible person.

5. Joel goes to . . . . university.

6. Frank has . . . . ugly car.

7. We are going to . . . . . . party.

8. My friend is . . . . intelligent person.

9. Nancy is . . . . teacher.

10. I have . . . . awesome friend.

11. Suzie is going to . . . . union meeting.

12. I will leave the library in . . . . . . hour.

EXERCISE 11 Answer these questions with **yes** or **no** responses.

Example: Is **the** bicycle yours?
Yes, **the** bicycle is mine.
No, **the** bicycle is not mine.

1. Is **the** tree tall?

   ....

2. Is this **a** good idea?

   ....

3. Do you live **an** hour from here?

   ....

4. Is this **a** good university?

   ....

5. Is **the** dog black?

   ....

6. Do you have **an** animal?

   ....

7. Is George **a** handsome man?

   ....

8. Did you eat **an** orange for breakfast?

   ....

9. Is **the** brown purse yours?

   . . . .

10. Do you have **a** computer?

    . . . .

Adverbs

Adverbs modify (describe) verbs, adjectives, and other adverbs. They usually answer: how, why, when, where or to what extent?

Common Adverbs

often, very, not, always, soon, most, quite, too, and most words ending in –ly.

Examples:

- Annery speaks English **perfectly**. (The adverb *perfectly* modifies the verb speaks.)
- Frank is **often** misunderstood. (The adverb *often* modifies the adjective *misunderstood*.)
- The child wakes up **very early**. (The adverb *very* modifies the adverb *early*.)

Changing Adjectives into Adverbs

Many adjectives can be transformed into adverbs by just adding *–ly*:

Adjectives	Adverbs
slow	slowly
prompt	promptly
harsh	harshly
confident	confidently
soft	softly
perfect	perfectly

EXERCISE 12 Underline the **adverb** in each sentence.

Example: Melissa sings (<u>beautifully</u>, beautiful).

1. Ana's car works (perfect, perfectly).

2. Ebony finished her project (quickly, quick).

3. The child speaks (softly, soft).

4. Alicia walks (confidently, confident).

5. Please close the door (soft, softly).

6. Erica walks too (rapidly, rapid).

7. Jason drives (slowly, slow).

8. Cynthia pronounces her words (careful, carefully).

9. The lion roars (loud, loudly).

10. The superstar entered the stage (graceful, gracefully).

EXERCISE 13 Rewrite each of the following sentences, and place the **adverb** at the **beginning** of the sentence.

Example: The boy **carefully** entered the burning building.
Carefully, the boy entered the burning building.

1. Johnny slowly crossed the street.

   . . . .

2. The cat quietly climbed the tree.

   . . . .

3. The hungry baby cried loudly.

   . . . .

4. The children quickly ran to school.

   . . . .

5. The minister preached eloquently.

   . . . .

6. The girl spoke brilliantly.

   . . . .

7. Antonio hurriedly left the house.

   . . . .

8. The basketball player skillfully passed the ball.

   . . . .

9. The teacher taught the lesson passionately.

   . . . .

10. The hotel employee spoke to the client harshly.

    . . . .

Comparative and Superlative Adverbs

Adverbs are compared in the same manner as adjectives. Most adverbs are two or more syllables and generally form the ***comparatives*** by adding ***more*** and the ***superlatives*** by adding ***most***.

Adverb	Comparative	Superlative
carefully	**more** carefully	**most** carefully
gracefully	**more** gracefully	**most** gracefully
energetically	**more** energetically	**most** energetically
tactfully	**more** tactfully	**most** tactfully
willingly	**more** willingly	**most** willingly
briefly	**more** briefly	**most** briefly
clearly	**more** clearly	**most** clearly
pleasantly	**more** pleasantly	**most** pleasantly

EXERCISE 14 Underline the correct **adverb** in parentheses.

1. Marcos completes his projects (more quickly, most quickly) than his sister.

2. Of the three speakers, Luis spoke (more clearly, most clearly).

3. Emily runs (most rapidly, more rapidly) than anyone on the track team.

4. Rafael thinks I sing (most loudly, more loudly) than the other singers.

5. Did Flora dance (more gracefully, most gracefully) than her peers?

6. Of the two singers, who sang (most eloquently, more eloquently)?

7. The younger sibling speaks (more positively, most positively) about learning math.

8. Does Martin work (more slowly, most slowly) than Katie?

9. Rebecca writes (more clearly, most clearly) than Ana.

10. Of the three sisters, who is the (more articulate, most articulate)?

Commonly Confused Adverbs: Good/Well

Good is an *adjective*. It can only be used to describe a noun or pronoun.

1. Use **good** *before* the noun it describes.

    Example: Nery is a **good** cook.

2. Use **good** *after* a form of the verb to be: am, is, are, was, were

    Example: He is a **good** friend.

3. Use **good** *after* a linking verb: seem, taste, look, grow, remain, stay, sound, appear

    Example: The soup tastes good.

Well, on the other hand, is an **adverb**. It describes an **action** verb and answers the question **how**.

Example: The chef cooks **well**. (How does the chef cook? He cooks **well**.)

EXERCISE 15 Underline the correct answer: good or well.

1. Juan is a (good, well) student.

2. Rewel speaks English (good, well).

3. Jose does his work (good, well).

4. My teacher seems as if she is not doing (good, well) today.

5. Antonio is a (good, well) preacher.

6. Rosanna is a (good, well) student.

7. Are you feeling (good, well) today?

8. The child is not doing (good, well).

9. Arturo delivered his presentation (good, well).

10. How (good, well) do you know Carmen?

EXERCISE 16 Answer these questions with **yes** or **no** responses.

Example: Is Eufemia a **good** grandmother?
Yes, Eufemia is a **good** grandmother.
No, Eufemia is not a **good** grandmother.

1. Does Alex speak Spanish **well**?

   ....

2. Is Bernardo a **good** driver?

   ....

3. Does Marlene speak Spanish **well**?

   ....

4. Is Jose a **good** deacon?

   ....

5. Does Virginia cook **well**?

   ....

6. Does Negro get along **well** with others?

   ....

7. Do Manuel and his sister get along **well**?

   . . . .

8. Is Pedro a **good** basketball player?

   . . . .

9. Is this a **good** restaurant?

   . . . .

10. Does Ernesto play the piano **well**?

    . . . .

Review

Correct the following paragraphs by crossing out the incorrect adjective or adverb, and then write the correct form above it. Every sentence does not have an error.

(1) Sabrina is the more recognized person in her family. (2) However, her brother Javier is the more intelligent one, but he does not think so. (3) He also has a interesting way of telling his family that he only gets well grades because he studies. (4) As soon as he arrives home from school, he does the more important thing, his homework. (5) Afterwards, he rests for a hour. (6) When he wakes up, he takes his dog for a walk. (7) This dog is the baddest dog on his block. (8) He barks loud at everything he sees, and he eats so greedy. (9) It is amazing to see how rapid he eats. (10) However, he protects his family good, so Javier adores him.

(1) Carlos is the more important employee on his job. (2) He is never late for work. (3) In fact, he is a hour early every day. (4) His supervisor thinks he does the better work of all the employees. (5) This might be true, but he also finds time to tell the funnier and more unusual stories I have ever heard. (6) He speaks very soft as he tells these stories. (7) No matter how busy an employee is, he or she pays attention and smiles when he tells his stories. (8) This stories are based on things that happened in his family. (9) He also dances good. (10) Carlos is definitely a unusual individual.

Answers

Exercise 1

1. new
2. loud
3. delicious
4. good
5. small
6. dangerous
7. tiny
8. good
9. silly
10. interesting

Exercise 2

Answers will vary

Exercise 3

Answers will vary.

Exercise 4

Answers will vary.

Exercise 5

1. better
2. most important
3. most expensive
4. funniest
5. most eloquent
6. worst
7. richest
8. more interesting
9. most efficient
10. biggest

Exercise 6

Answers will vary

Exercise 7

	Adjective	Comparative	Superlative
1.	young	younger	youngest
2.	marvelous	more marvelous	most marvelous
3.	silly	sillier	silliest
4.	common	more common	most common
5.	bad	worse	worst
6.	hot	hotter	hottest
7.	responsible	more responsible	most responsible
8.	beautiful	more beautiful	most beautiful
9.	intelligent	more intelligent	most intelligent
10.	great	greater	greatest

Exercise 8

1. taller
2. best
3. hottest
4. smartest
5. wettest
6. largest
7. worst
8. drier
9. more
10. highest
11. most
12. best

Exercise 9

Answers will vary

Exercise 10

1. a
2. a
3. a
4. an
5. a
6. an
7. a
8. an
9. a
10. an
11. a
12. an

Exercise 11

Answers will vary

Exercise 12

1. perfectly
2. quickly
3. softly
4. confidently
5. softly
6. rapidly
7. slowly
8. carefully
9. loudly
10. gracefully

Exercise 13

1. Slowly, Johnny crossed the street.
2. Quietly, the cat climbed the tree.
3. Loudly, the hungry baby cried.
4. Quickly, the children ran to school.
5. Eloquently, the minister preached.
6. Brilliantly, the girl spoke.
7. Hurriedly, Antonio left the house.
8. Skillfully, the basketball player passed the ball.
9. Passionately, the teacher taught the lesson.
10. Harshly, the hotel employee spoke to the client.

Exercise 14

Underline the correct adverb in parentheses.

1. more quickly
2. most clearly
3. more rapidly
4. more loudly
5. more gracefully
6. more eloquently
7. more positively
8. more slowly
9. more clearly
10. most articulate

Exercise 15

1. good
2. well
3. well
4. well
5. good
6. good
7. good
8. well
9. well
10. well

Exercise 16

Answers will vary

Review

(1) Sabrina is the **most** recognized person in her family. (2) However, her brother Javier is the **most** intelligent one, but he does not think so. (3) He also has **an** interesting way of telling his family that he only gets **good** grades because he studies. (4) As soon as he arrives home from school, he does the important thing, his homework. (5) Afterwards, he rests for **an** hour. (6) When he wakes up, he takes his dog for a walk. (7) This dog is the **worst** dog on his block. (8) He barks **loudly** at everything he sees, and he eats so **greedily**. (9) It is amazing to see how he eats. (10) However, he protects his family **well**, so Javier adores him.

(1) Carlos is the **most** important employee on his job. (2) He is never late for work. (3) In fact, he is **an** hour early every day. (4) His supervisor thinks he does the **best** work of all the employees. (5) This might be true, but he also finds time to tell the **funniest** and **most** unusual stories I have ever heard. (6) He speaks very **softly** as he tells these stories. (7) No matter how busy an employee is, he or she pays attention and smiles when he tells his stories. (8) **These** stories are based on things that happened in his family. (9) He also dances **well**. (10) Carlos is definitely **an** unusual individual.

About The Author

Merlene J. Purkiss earned a bachelor's degree in liberal studies from Barry University and then a master's degree in English Education from Nova Southeastern University. An author of four English textbooks, she is a senior associate professor at Miami Dade College, where she has worked with language arts students for nearly 40 years. She is also the founder and president of a non-profit organization called Alfa Outreach Ministries, Inc., which specifically targets impoverished families in Jamaica, Haiti, Dominican Republic, and South Florida.

Purkiss' main purpose in life is to inspire the young minds she teaches and the struggling families she encounters to rise above their circumstances and achieve greatness. She believes that God has created us for good works, but sometimes we allow life's circumstances to deter us from germinating our dreams and passions.

www.ingramcontent.com/pod-product-compliance
Lightning Source LLC
Chambersburg PA
CBHW051428070526
44584CB00023B/3628